HISTORY IN DEPTH

FACTORY REFORM

John Patrick

MACMILLAN EDUCATION

First published 1987
Reprinted 1987

Published by
MACMILLAN EDUCATION LTD
Houndmills, Basingstoke, Hampshire RG21 2XS
and London
Companies and representatives throughout the world

Printed in Hong Kong

British Library Cataloguing in Publication Data
Patrick, John, *1931-*
Factory reform. — (History in depth)
1. Labour and labouring classes — Great
Britain — History 2. Factory system
— Great Britain — History 3. Work
environment — Great Britain — History
I. Title II. Series
331.2′0941 HD8389
ISBN 0-333-40918-3

CONTENTS

Acknowledgements

The author and publishers wish to acknowledge, with thanks, the following photographic sources:

Aerofilms pp 11, 47; BBC Hulton Picture Library pp 5, 9, 13, 20, 23, 29, 34, 41, 46; Royal Commission on the Ancient and Historical Monuments of Scotland (copyright reserved) p 12; Mansell Collection pp 6, 8, 15, 18, 25, 31, 35, 39, 42 bottom, 44; National Union of Teachers p 42 top; Topham Picture Library p 32.

The publishers have made every effort to trace the copyright holders, but if they have inadvertently overlooked any, they will be pleased to make the necessary arrangements at the first opportunity.

PREFACE

The study of history is exciting, whether in a good story well told, a mystery solved by the judicious unravelling of clues, or a study of the men, women and children whose fears and ambitions, successes and tragedies make up the collective memory of mankind.

This series aims to reveal this excitement to pupils through a set of topic books on important historical subjects from the Middle Ages to the present day. Each book contains four main elements: a narrative and descriptive text, lively and relevant illustrations, extracts of contemporary evidence, and questions for further thought and work. Involvement in these elements should provide an adventure which will bring the past to life in the imagination of the pupil.

Each book is also designed to develop the knowledge, skills and concepts so essential to a pupil's growth. It provides a wide, varying introduction to the evidence available on each topic. In handling this evidence, pupils will increase their understanding of basic historical concepts such as causation and change, as well as of more advanced ideas such as revolution and democracy. In addition, their use of basic study skills will be complemented by more sophisticated historical skills such as the detection of bias and the formulation of opinion.

The intended audience for the series is pupils of eleven to sixteen years; it is expected that the earlier topics will be introduced in the first three years of secondary school, while the nineteenth and twentieth century topics are directed towards first examinations.

1 THE DOMESTIC SYSTEM

Making cloth in the eighteenth century

Samuel Bamford was born in Lancashire in 1788. As a boy he worked for his uncle, who was a weaver. Many years later, in his autobiography, he described his uncle's home. It consisted of 'one principal room, called "the house". On the same floor with this was a loom-shop capable of containing four looms, and in the rear of the house on the same floor, were a small kitchen and a buttery. Over the house and loom-shop were [bed]chambers'.

At the beginning of the nineteenth century Thomas Cooper lived in Gainsborough in Lincolnshire with his widowed mother. She dyed cloth for a living. Their house consisted of 'but one chamber and one lower room, and the last-named was at once parlour, kitchen, and dye-house. Two large coppers were set in one part of it, and my mother was at work, amidst steam and sweat, all the day long'.

In the eighteenth century making cloth was Britain's most important industry. Woollen cloth was manufactured in most parts of Britain. In addition, linen was made in Scotland, and raw cotton, imported from India, was made into cloth in the area around Manchester.

Two women spinning. Two carding combs lie on the floor between them

In order to make cloth, the raw wool, cotton or flax has to be combed out or 'carded'. Then it is spun into threads, which are woven together on a loom to form the cloth. Finally, the cloth is 'finished' by being pounded in water to clean and shrink it. It is now ready to be dyed.

Spinning and weaving

Spinning was usually done by women. John Younger, who grew up on a farm towards the end of the eighteenth century, remembered how his mother used 'to rise very early, even on cold winter mornings, for the purpose of spinning yarn.... The boom of her large [wheel], and the birr of her small wheel were music to my young ear on awakening'. The large wheel was used to spin wool. The small wheel was used for linen.

Weaving was traditionally man's work, although by 1800 many women had taken it up. The weaver had to stretch out one set of threads, called the warp, on his loom, and then made the cloth by passing another thread, called the woof, through the warp at right angles. The warp had to be made of strong, thick thread. The woof was often thinner and weaker. The woof was carried on a shuttle which, at the beginning of the eighteenth century, was threaded through the warp by hand. On narrow looms the weaver leaned over the front of his loom to thread the shuttle through, but broad looms required two people, one on each side, who passed the shuttle to and fro between them. There had to be more spinners than weavers because it took four or five spinners to keep a weaver supplied with thread.

An 18th century French engraving of a hand-loom weaver at work

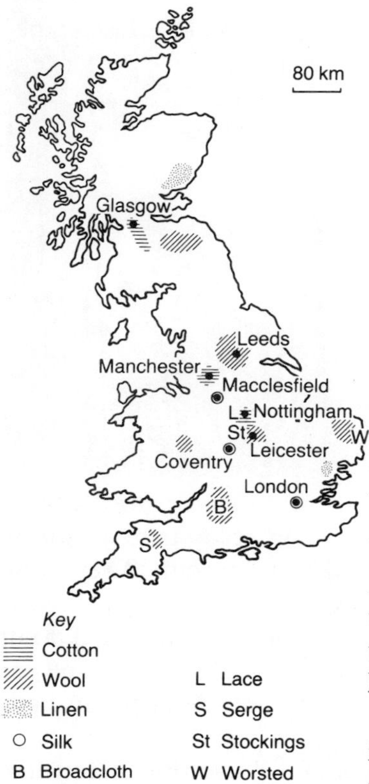

Areas where cloth was produced in the 18th century

Using the evidence

1 According to the evidence quoted here, did cloth workers:
  a) go out to factories to work
  b) work at home in outbuildings
  c) work inside the house?

2 What source of power did the workers use?

3 Look at the pictures of the loom and the spinning wheels. Do you think they would have been costly to buy? Would they be difficult to repair?

4 Would it have been easy or difficult to set up as a spinner or weaver in the eighteenth century? Give reasons for your answer.

Very few families made their entire living from spinning or weaving. Many also had land to farm. In 1751 a Lancashire boy told a traveller that he and his father 'wove woollen cloth both for their clothing and to sell'; his father also rented a farm for £6 a year, on which he kept 'a horse, three cows and 40 sheep'.

Other cloth workers, who owned no land, worked as farm labourers in the summer, bringing their wives and children to help with the hay and corn harvests when farmers needed all the labour they could get. But in winter, when there was less work on the farms, the labourers and their families spent their time spinning and weaving.

Putting out

Some spinners only produced enough thread to make clothes for their families, but many worked for cloth merchants. Every week the merchant called to deliver a quantity of raw wool. At the same time he collected the thread the spinners had made during the past week, and paid them for their work. In the same way he delivered thread to weavers for them to make into cloth, collected finished cloth, and paid them for each piece they had made. This system of handing out work for people to do was known as 'putting out', and the spinners and weavers were said to be on 'piece work', because they were paid for each piece of work they did, and not according to the number of hours they worked.

Children's work

In all working families, children were expected to help as soon as they were able. When Daniel Defoe, the journalist and author, visited Yorkshire at the beginning of the eighteenth century, he noticed that even four-year-olds had to earn their keep. In all parts of the country

Weavers' houses in Bethnal Green, London. The upstairs workshops had large windows to give the weavers plenty of light

parish officials in charge of paying allowances to needy families would not pay any benefit for children over eight years old. They were thought to be old enough to earn a living.

Most people accepted child labour as quite normal, so they did not bother to find out how many hours a day boys and girls worked, or what effect this had on their health. However, some descriptions have survived.

According to Richard Oastler, the agent of a Yorkshire landowner:

It was the custom for the children at that time to mix learning their trade with other instruction and with amusement, and they learned their trades . . . by having a little work to do, and then some little time for instruction, and they were generally under the immediate care of their parents. . . . There were filial affection and parental feeling, and not over-labour.

Samuel Bamford, the Lancashire weaver's nephew, remembered:

Some two or three weeks before Christmas it was the custom in families to apportion to each boy or girl weaver a certain quantity of work which was to be done ere his or her holidays commenced. An extra quantity was generally undertaken to be performed. . . . In most families a peck or a strike of malt would be brewed; spiced bread or potato custard would be made, and probably an extra piece of beef and some good old cheese would be laid in store, not to be touched until the work was done. The work then went on merrily. Play hours were nearly given up, and whole nights would be spent at the loom, the weavers occasionally striking up a hymn or Christmas carol in chorus . . . to keep ourselves from sleep, and we chorused 'Christians awake' when we ourselves were almost gone to sleep.

S. Bamford: *Early Days*, 1849

peck: a peck of malt made 20 litres of strong ale
strike: probably 2 pecks

Mary Thorpe, of Bulwell near Nottingham, told a visitor to the district what happened in poor families:

Little children begin here to work at stitching gloves when very young. My little sister, now five and a half, can stitch a good many little fingers and is very clever, having been at it for two years. She used to stand on a stool so as to be able to see up at the candle on the table. Little children are kept up shamefully late if there is work – often till 11 and 12. Mothers will pin them to their knee to keep them to their work and give them a slap to keep them awake. If the children are pinned so, they cannot fall when they are slapped or go to sleep.

Hannah Hawkins, a 16-year-old factory worker, backed up Mary Thorpe's story. In 1833 she said:

Before I came here, I have been employed in seaming gloves at home along with my mother. Never have done anything else. Earned from 3s. to 4s. a week at that. Used to begin work at seven and work until nine at night. Two hours at meals. Used to do that regularly. . . . My health was not that good.

Before 1972 British money was reckoned in pounds, shillings and pence (£-s.-d.). There were 12 pence in a shilling and 20 shillings in a pound. Between 1820 and 1840 the price of a 2kg loaf averaged about 9d., and a small house cost about 2s. a week to rent.

Boys were not expected to spin or sew. If they had no loom, they might stick heads on pins for a living. A doctor said that:

Unhappy children . . . have to sit twelve hours a day at a table, with their bodies continuously bent in the form of a little c, their eyes fixed upon pin-heads and with hands and feet in continuous motion.

This boy is using a foot-operated machine to fix tags to laces

---

Using the evidence

1 Which of the accounts of children's work gives the most favourable impression of how children were treated? Which gives the worst impression? Give reasons for your answer.

2 Which of the five witnesses would you expect to know most about working children? And which would you expect to know the least? Give reasons for your answer.

3 Basing your answer on the evidence given here, which of the following statements do you think most likely to be true:
a) Most working children were always well-treated by their parents.
b) Most working children were sometimes treated badly.
c) Most working children were treated badly most of the time.
Give reasons for your choice. Why is it difficult for us now to be certain how most children were treated?

4 Read Samuel Bamford's evidence again. Does he seem to have enjoyed the time he spent working for his uncle as a weaver?
Imagine you are a young weaver in a similar situation. Using the information given by Bamford, write a letter to your parents to convince them that you are being badly treated.

---

2 THE FIRST CLOTH MILLS

Spinning and weaving machines

In 1721 Britain's wool merchants persuaded Parliament to pass an Act forbidding the importation of cotton cloth, because too many people were buying it in preference to woollen cloth. After the Act had been passed, shippers brought in raw cotton instead. This had to be processed in Britain, and the spinners and weavers could not cope with the extra work. As a result, inventors devised several machines to speed up spinning and weaving. Details of their inventions are given in the following tables.

Improvements in weaving		
Machine	*Description*	*Importance*
Flying shuttle Invented by John Kay in 1733. 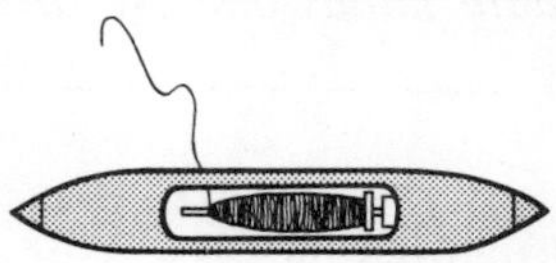	System which threw the shuttle from one side of the loom to the other, automatically.	Doubled weavers' output. Enabled one man to weave broad-cloth on his own. In common use by 1760.
Power loom Invented by Edmund Cartwright. Patented in 1786. 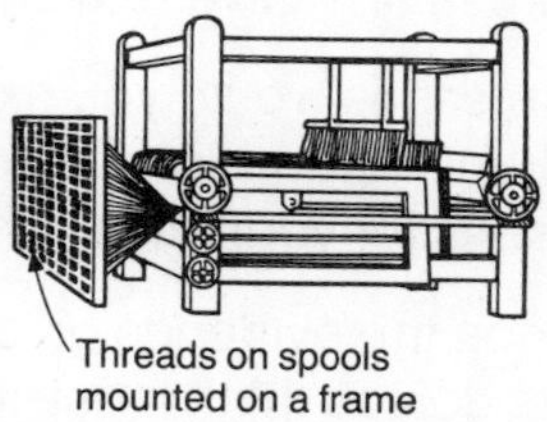 	First practical power-driven loom.	Not in common use until 1820. Enabled unskilled workers to weave large quantities of plain cloth.

Improvements in spinning		
Machine	*Description*	*Importance*
Spinning jenny Invented by James Hargreaves. Patented in 1770. 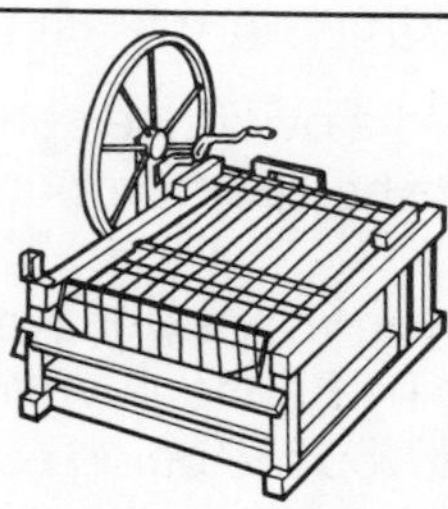	Small, cheap, clumsy, hand-powered spinning machine with several spindles.	Enabled one spinner to produce several threads at once. Produced thin, uneven thread. Needed no skill to operate it.

Machine	Description	Importance
Water frame Invented by Richard Arkwright. Patented in 1775. 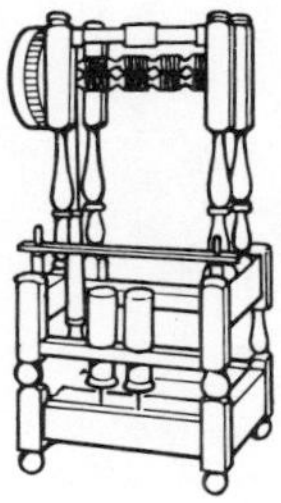	Stiff, heavy spinning machine, using rollers to produce several threads at once.	Produced thick thread. Needed horse or water power to drive it. Needed no skill to operate it.
Spinning mule Invented by Samuel Crompton in 1779. 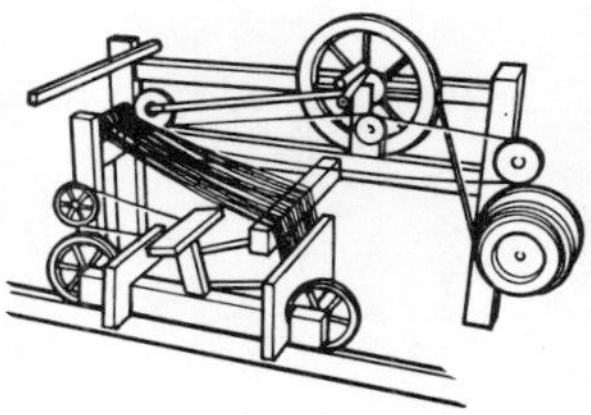	A complicated machine, using features from both the jenny and the water frame.	Could produce thread of any thickness. Needed a skilled operator.

The water wheel at Arkwright's cotton mill at Cromford in Derbyshire. This wheel once provided the power to run all the machines in the factory

Using the evidence

1 Why was it necessary to invent machines to speed up spinning after 1760?

2 Which was the first spinning machine that could not be used in people's homes? Why was this?

3 'Mule' spinners were always well paid. Why was this?

4 Which machine could produce warp for the loom cheaply?

5 Which machine could produce woof for the loom cheaply?

6 Which machine could produce both warp and woof? (Look up warp and woof in Chapter 1 if necessary.)

Water mills

The first spinning machines were comparatively small. In 1780 jennies had only eight or ten spindles, but by 1800 some had more than a hundred. These larger machines needed power to drive them. Water power was cheap and reliable, so manufacturers set up factories wherever they could find a stream with a steady flow to turn a water wheel and drive their machines.

Many of the most suitable streams flowed through isolated valleys. For instance, in 1783 David Dale found a good site for a cotton mill on the River Clyde in Scotland, several kilometres from the nearest town. He decided to build a mill there, but found that very few people lived within walking distance, so there was nobody to operate his machines.

Woodside Cotton Mill near Aberdeen was powered by a water wheel which was housed underneath the middle of the mill building

He built houses for workers close to his factory, but could not persuade anyone to come and live in them. Many other manufacturers faced the same problem.

Parish apprentices

Dale's mill was equipped with water frames, which could easily be operated by children. Dale knew that in every large town there were orphan children under the care of the local parish authority, so he wrote to the authorities in several towns, offering to take these children as apprentices – he would give them clothes, board and lodging until they were 21, and in return they would work in his factory. The authorities were glad that someone was offering to take the orphans off their hands, and willingly sent them to learn how to spin cotton in Dale's mill. Other manufacturers followed Dale's example, and by 1800 thousands of orphan apprentices were working in spinning mills.

There are many accounts of how the apprentices were treated. Feargus O'Connor, a well-known politician, said in a speech in Oldham in 1836 that the guard of the London to Manchester coach had told him that 'scores of poor children, taken from workhouses, or kidnapped in the streets... used to be brought down by that coach to Manchester and slid into a cellar in Mosley Street as if they had been stones'.

John Aikin, a Manchester doctor, wrote:

Children of very tender age are employed; many of them collected from the workhouses in London and Westminster, and trans-

ported in crowds, as apprentices to masters resident many hundred miles distant, where they serve unknown, unprotected and forgotten.... These children are usually too long confined to work in close rooms, often during the whole night: the air they breathe from the oil, etc., employed in the machinery, and other circumstances is injurious; little regard is paid to their cleanliness.

J. Aikin: *A Description of the Country from Thirty to Forty Miles Round Manchester*, 1975

William Lockhart was a landowner who lived near Dale's mill. He visited it frequently, and in 1793 he wrote a description of it. He said there were 1 334 employees in all, 795 of whom were boys and girls. He described the apprentices' living and working conditions:

The diet consists of oatmeal porridge with milk... twice a day, as much as they can take, barley broth for dinner, made with good fresh beef every day; and as much beef is boiled as will allow 7 oz a-piece each day to one half of the children, the other half get cheese and bread after their broth, so that they dine alternately upon cheese and butchermeat, with barley bread and potatoes; and now and then in the proper season they have a dinner of herrings and potatoes. They, as well as the others, begin work at six in the morning, are allowed half an hour for dinner, and quit work at 7 at night; after which they attend the school at the expense of the proprietor till 9. They sleep in well aired rooms, three in a bed; and proper care is taken to remove those under any disease to separate apartments.

Children helping to wind cotton thread from spindles onto frames ready for the weavers

Robert Owen, David Dale's son-in-law, gave more details about the apprentices. They were:

> *. . . generally from the age of five and six, to seven and eight, . . . because Mr Dale could not . . . obtain them at a more advanced period of life; if he did not take them at those ages, he could not obtain them at all. . . . Although those children were very well fed, well clothed, well lodged, and very great care taken of them when out of the mills, their growth and their minds were materially injured by being employed at those ages within the cotton mills for eleven hours and a half per day. . . . Their limbs were generally deformed. Their growth was stunted.*

Sir Robert Peel, who owned a cloth mill at Ratcliff Bridge near Manchester, was too busy to visit it often. But in 1800 he noticed:

remuneration: pay

> *. . . the uniform appearance of bad health, and in many cases of stunted growth of the children. The hours of work were regulated by the . . . overseer, whose remuneration depending on the quantity of work done, he was often induced to make the poor children work excessive hours, and to stop their complaints by trifling bribes.*

In 1814 John Moss was employed to look after the apprentices at Backbarrow Mill in Lancashire. In 1816 he gave evidence to a Parliamentary committee. Here are some of the questions asked by the committee members, and the answers Moss gave:

'What were the hours of work?' — 'From 5 o'clock in the morning till 8 at night all the year through.'
'What time was allowed for meals?' — 'Half an hour for breakfast and half an hour for dinner.'
'What time did they rise from bed?' — 'I always got them up at half-past four to get them ready for the mill by five.'
'At what hour did they go to bed?' — 'Nine o'clock was their hour.'
'Were any of the children injured by the machinery?' — 'Very frequently. Very often their fingers were crushed, and one had his arm broken.'
'Were any of the children deformed?' — 'Yes, several; there were two or three that were very crooked.'
'As the children grew up, did they in general appear to be healthy, or otherwise?' — 'There were some who were very healthy children, and there were others that were sickly looking.'
'How were the children lodged?' — 'When I first went there, their bedding was very bad. They had only a blanket to lie on, and a thin blanket on top, and a horse cover.'
'Could they be preserved cleanly with sleeping only on blankets?' — 'They were not altogether clean.'
'Were the children fed well?' — 'Yes, very well.'

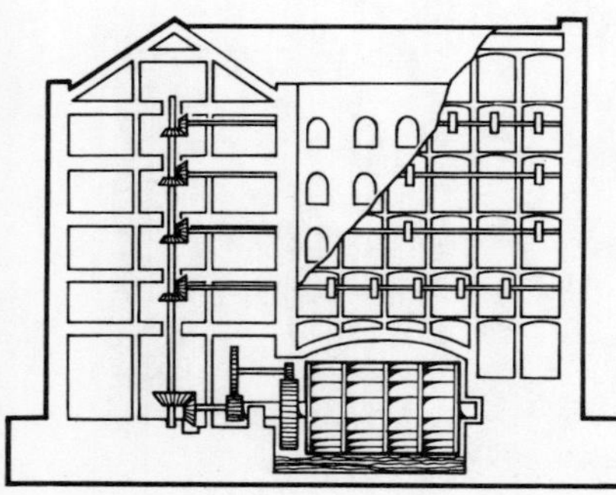
The working parts of a water mill

The settlement at New Lanark. The mill and the workers' houses were all built in the same style

Using the evidence

1 Does O'Connor's speech contain reliable evidence of the way in which apprentices were treated? Justify your answer.

2 Why is the evidence given by (a) Robert Peel and Robert Owen, and (b) John Moss, particularly useful?

3 Write an account of how you think most apprentices in cloth mills were treated, including their hours of work, food, lodging, etc. In this piece you must not make any general statement (e.g. apprentices worked 15 hours a day) unless it is supported by at least two of the people quoted above.

4 Are there any features of the apprentices' life which would be unacceptable today, but which people in the eighteenth century would have taken for granted? (See also Chapter 1.)

5 Imagine you are a reporter touring cloth mills in Lancashire. You are shocked by what you have seen. Write an article to convince your readers that apprentices are disgracefully treated.

The Health and Morals of Apprentices Act, 1802

Sir Robert Peel was an MP as well as a factory owner. He thought that many parish apprentices working in cloth mills were badly treated and unhealthy. There was an outbreak of fever at his own mill, and he heard of other outbreaks elsewhere. Most apprentices had no relatives to speak up for them, and Peel decided that a law ought to be passed to protect them. In 1802 he persuaded Parliament to pass the Health and

Morals of Apprentices Act. This Act limited the apprentices' working day to 12 hours, and forbade employers to make them work at night. For the first four years of their apprenticeship, the boys and girls had to spend part of their working day at school. Factories had to be whitewashed regularly, and properly ventilated. Separate sleeping accommodation had to be provided for boys and girls, and apprentices were not to sleep more than two in a bed. Local magistrates were ordered to appoint two 'visitors' to inspect the mills, and mill owners who broke the law could be fined up to £10.

In 1816 a Parliamentary committee tried to find out how well the Act was being enforced. John Moss, the Backbarrow overseer, said he had never heard of the Act. Richard Arkwright, the owner of Cromford Mill in Derbyshire, said:

> *The Act has not been followed up, with respect to the visiting of magistrates, for these thirteen years. I think they visited my mills at Cromford twice.*

William Evans, a Manchester magistrate, told the committee:

> *I certainly was aware of the existence of an Act for the regulation of cotton mills [but] . . . I had not the curiosity, though I have read as many Acts of Parliament as most persons, to read that [one] till I came into this room.*

Using the evidence

1 To judge by the information given in Chapter 1, do you think most people at the time would have thought the rules laid down by Peel's Act:
a) still too hard on the apprentices
b) about right
c) hard on the factory owners?
Give reasons for your answer.

2 What is there in the evidence to suggest that the 1802 Act was not properly enforced?

3 Why is it surprising that William Evans had never read the Act?

After 1800 the number of parish apprentices employed in factories began to fall. When apprentices grew up, many married and set up house close to the mill where they were working. When their children were old enough they sent them to work in the mill. By 1820 it cost five shillings a week to keep an apprentice, while a ten-year-old factory worker living at home was only paid three shillings a week. So mill owners encouraged their former apprentices to stay by providing low-rent houses for them to live in. Gradually villages grew up round the isolated mills.

3

THE STEAM MILLS

In the eighteenth century most cloth mills were driven by water wheels – the cheapest and most reliable source of power available. But by 1800 James Watt had developed reliable steam engines which provided enough power to drive all the machines in a factory.

Steam engines		
1712	Newcomen's steam pump.	Only the down stroke was powered. The cylinder was heated up and cooled down between each stroke. Could only be used as a pump.
1776	James Watt's separate condenser. 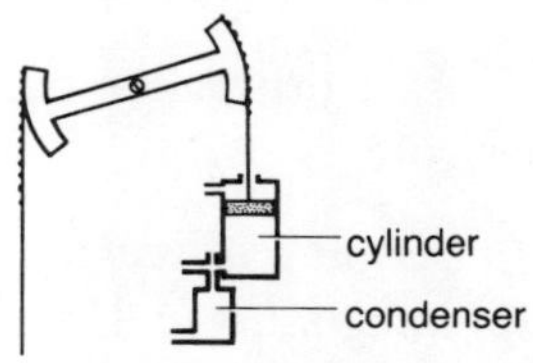	Enabled the cylinder to be kept hot all the time. Speeded up the engine.
1782	Watt's double-acting engine.	Used steam to drive the piston both up and down the cylinder.
1782	Sun and planet wheel. 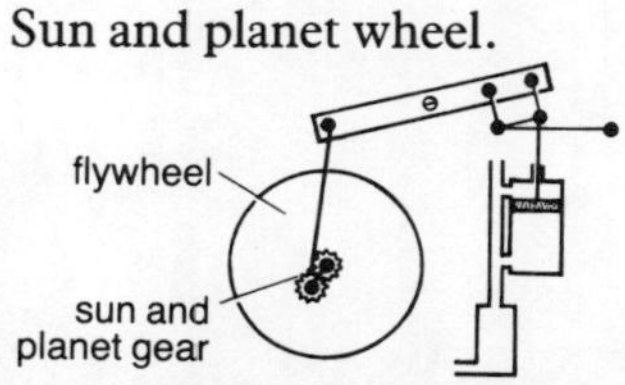	Enabled steam engines to be used to drive machinery.
1785	First steam engine installed in a cotton mill, at Papplewick in Nottinghamshire.	
1800	More than 100 steam engines in use in cotton mills.	

Manufacturers using steam engines no longer had to build their mills where there was a good flow of water. Instead they put them in or near towns, such as Manchester, where there were plenty of people to work in the mills.

Large steam mills

In 1814 J.G. May, a German factory inspector, visited Manchester to see the new mills. He wrote:

> *There are hundreds of factories in Manchester which are five or six storeys high. At the side of each factory there is a great chimney which belches forth black smoke and indicates the presence of the powerful steam engines. The smoke from the chimneys forms a great cloud which can be seen for miles around the town. . . .*
>
> *The visitor who is armed with letters of introduction has no difficulty in gaining admission to factories in Manchester. . . . In the large spinning mills machines of different kinds stand in rows like regiments in an army. . . . Two machines, each with 300 spindles, face each other. The carriages of these machines are moved in one direction by steam and in the other direction by hand. This is done by an adult worker who stands in between the two machines. Broken threads are repaired by children who stand at either end of the machines.*
>
> Quoted in W.O. Henderson's book, *Industrial Britain under the Regency*, 1968

A Swiss clothmaker named Escher also visited Manchester in 1814. He wrote:

> *In a short walk which lasted only fifteen minutes I counted over sixty spinning mills in Manchester. . . . In spite of all the smoke they create one must admire the steam engines here. . . . One shudders when one sees the piston of an engine going up and one realises that a force of 60 to 80 horse power is being generated. . . . A single steam engine*

Steam-powered mills in Union Street, Manchester

frequently operates 40,000 to 50,000 spindles in a mill which has eight or nine floors. . . . In a single street in Manchester there are more spindles than in the whole of Switzerland. . . . The spinning mills are now working until 8 p.m. by gaslight. Unless one has seen it for oneself it is impossible to imagine how grand is the sight of a big cotton mill when a facade of 256 windows is lit as if the brightest sunshine were streaming through the windows.

Quoted in W.O. Henderson's book, as above

A steam mill with 50 000 spindles cost at least £80 000 to build. It would employ 750 workers who could produce about 100 500 kilometres of thread a day – enough to go nearly three times round the world.

In 1823 a Home Office inspector visited a steam mill at Tyldesley, near Manchester. He reported that it was well ventilated, with a temperature of 72 degrees. He went on:

flue: fluff

The machinery in this factory and also the steam engine were of highly polished steel and brass, and the wood principally of mahogany, and the floors and every part of it remarkably clean and neat. No flue was perceptible, the atmosphere was pure; and the workpeople appear to have every comfort. Home Office papers

---

Using the evidence

1 Study the illustration of steam mills in Union Street, Manchester. Does it correspond with May's description? Apart from the actual mill buildings, what other features shown in the picture were probably connected with the work of the mill?

2 What other sources, apart from pictures and written descriptions, might supply evidence of what early nineteenth century mills looked like?

3 Imagine you were visiting mills in Manchester at the beginning of the nineteenth century. What signs might you have seen indicating that some mill owners took a pride in their mills? Why might the mill owners have been proud of them?

Smaller mills

There were also many small mills in the Manchester area, where steam engines had been added to existing factories. Home Office inspectors visited several in 1823. At Horwich they went to Taylor and Urcher's Mill. They reported:

On entering we were nearly suffocated with the heat and a most intolerable stench; and on inspecting the interior (though it was with

A small, steam-powered wool mill at Morley, near Leeds

difficulty we did so) we found the whole building in a truly disgraceful state. The rooms were exceedingly low and crowded with workmen. The ceilings were literally covered with cotton and dust, and from the small number of windows in each room, we cannot conceive it possible for the children or the workmen to have sufficient air to enjoy good health.

At Ormerod's Mill in Westleigh they found the temperature:

effluvia: vapour

. . . not much under eighty degrees. The smells arising from the rancid effluvia and the confined perspiration of bodies labouring in heated rooms, from coarse oil with the general want of cleanliness caused a very powerful nausea to persons entering the buildings.

Home Office papers

A twentieth century view

At the beginning of the twentieth century Edward Carpenter, a poet born in 1844, gave his idea of what an early nineteenth century steam mill was like. He referred to:

. . . the great oblong ugly factory, in five or six tiers, all windows, alive with lights on a dark winter's morning, and again with the same lights in the evening; and all day within, the thump and scream of the machinery, and the thick smell of hot oil and cotton fluff, and crowds of drab-faced, drab-dressed men and women and children – the mill-hands – going to and fro or serving the machines.

E. Carpenter: *Towards Democracy*, part IV, 1902

Using the evidence

1. Can you suggest why the Home Office officials found it difficult to inspect Taylor and Urcher's Mill at Horwich, while J.G. May found it easy to visit the larger mills?
2. What differences were noticed between large and small mills?
3. Is Edward Carpenter's description of a cotton mill a primary or a secondary source? Justify your answer. Did Carpenter approve or disapprove of factories? What words or expressions does he use that make his views clear? How far does his account agree with the evidence contained in other extracts in this chapter?

Children in the mills

Owners of steam-powered mills liked to employ children. They were easy to train, needed less pay than adults and, being small, could move easily between and under the machines. In spinning mills children carried cotton to the spinning frames from the carding machines where it was prepared, while a few were employed to clear away scraps of cotton which gradually accumulated under the machines. But most children were 'piecers'. They had to watch the machines and every time a thread broke one of them had to stop the spinning spindle, find the end of thread on it and tie it to the other loose end – and all this was done while the machine was still running. If the cotton was good and the machine was running smoothly, piecers might not have much to do, but sometimes they were very busy. In 1833 Sir David Barry, a Scottish doctor, watched two 13-year-old piecers at work in a flax mill. He wrote:

> *One attended to sixty spindles, the other to fifty. It is quite impossible to give an adequate notion of the quickness with which these girls joined their broken ends of thread. There is no standing still; every muscle is in action, and that in quick succession.*

The work of these children was essential to keep the machinery running. When they stopped work, the machines also had to stop, so children employed in the mills worked the same hours as adults.

'Free' child workers

Children who were sent out to work by their parents were not apprentices, so the 1802 Act did not apply to them. This troubled Sir Robert Peel. He did not mind if children worked long hours at home under the control of their parents, but he thought it wrong for them to have to work more than 12 hours a day in a factory supervised by a

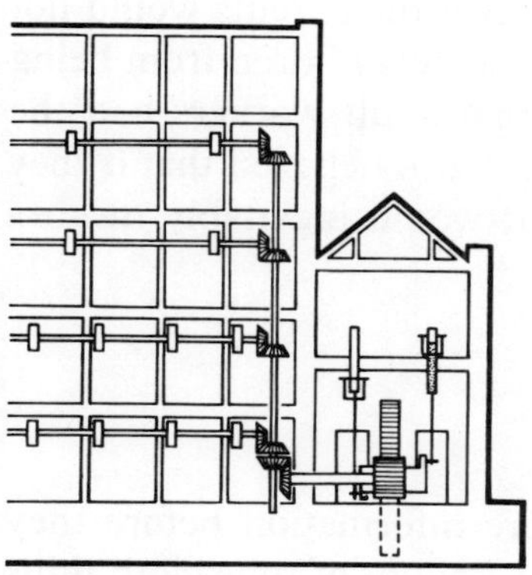

The working parts of a steam mill

This 20-horsepower steam engine dates from about 1825. It was more compact, more complicated and more powerful than the one which powered the mill at Morley

foreman or factory owner whose only interest was in keeping them working as long and hard as they could.

In 1815 Peel proposed a Bill to limit the hours worked by all factory children. This made many MPs uneasy; they thought it was up to parents to complain if they considered that their children were being made to work too hard. Others believed that if the parents would not do anything about it, Parliament ought to protect children from being overworked. But almost all MPs agreed that adult workers had the right to work for as long as they liked. They also believed that if they limited the hours that children worked, it would inevitably mean a shorter working day for adults.

The 1816 committee

MPs decided that they needed much more information before they dared to make a law which might limit the amount of time cloth mills could stay open, so they appointed a committee to interview witnesses connected with the cloth trade.

In the 18th century children printed patterns on cloth by hand. The girl is mixing the colour. The boy is using a wooden block to print the pattern

A *The mill owners' evidence*

Archibald Buchanan owned several cloth mills in Scotland, where nine-year-olds worked 12 hours a day, earning up to two shillings a week. He was asked:

> *'Do you ever receive complaints from the parents of the number of hours the children work?' — [He replied:] 'I do not recollect any complaint on that subject.'*
> *'Are the parents generally very desirous to send their children to you or not?' — 'Very desirous.'*

The committee also interviewed Henry Hollins, a cotton spinner from Mansfield in Nottinghamshire:

> *'Is there any bodily labour or exertion whatever used by children employed in your mill?' — 'Certainly nothing to be called labour.'*
> *'Are the children employed in such work as could not well be done by persons that are grown up?' — 'It is . . . better done by children. We could not afford to employ grown-up persons.'*
> *'What difference do you observe in the . . . health of the children employed in your manufactory, and the children in the neighbourhood belonging to farmers and agriculturalists?' — 'Perhaps they may be in a trifling degree inferior in point of appearance, but I think they are equally healthy.'*

Henry Houldsworth, a Glasgow spinner whose factory was in operation for 12 hours 50 minutes a day, was asked:

carriage: see illustration on page 31

> *'Are the children who attend the spinning department incessantly employed?' — 'Their attention is required every three quarters of a minute, or a minute, but between the time of the carriage coming out and going in, they have nothing to do.'*
> *'Do they sit down during that time?' — 'They have no means allowed them to sit down, and it would be scarcely worth their while from the space of time, but they generally have books in their bosom to read.'*
> *'Do they appear dull and fatigued at work?' — 'No, they do not; they are generally either reading, or singing, or talking to their neighbours.'*
> *'Have you observed that the growth of children in your factories has been stunted?' — 'No, I have not.'*
> *'Have you observed that any of them have been deformed, from standing long?' — 'No, I never observed a deformed child in the mill, that I know of.'*

B *Other witnesses*

The committee interviewed a number of doctors. They asked Mr Ashley Cooper, a surgeon:

> *'At what age may children, without endangering their health, be admitted to close labour for thirteen hours a day?' — 'I think at no age.'*

'Do you think that children from seven to ten years of age can be employed more than ten hours a day without injury to their health?' — 'I think not.'

Most of the doctors interviewed agreed with Ashley Cooper.

The MPs also called various witnesses who visited cloth mills. George Gould, a Manchester cloth merchant, told them that mill children looked:

. . . younger than they are, and the same remark has been made to me by others. Generally speaking, their appearance is delicate, and less healthy than that of children confined to fewer hours of labour in the day. Many of them, the younger children specially, are very badly clothed and dirty. . . . The youngest children, moreover, from inattention and carelessness, often become crippled by being entangled in the machinery.

Theodore Price, a magistrate, spoke of visiting Emscot Mill, near Warwick, where children worked 12½ hours a day.

hectic: feverish

I thought the children short in stature, and they had a hectic appearance, probably from constant work and the warmth of the room. They were going backwards and forwards, twisting the threads when they broke, and they were obliged to move quickly across a large room. There was a moisture about their faces, and they appeared hectic.

C *Evidence the committee never heard*

There is other evidence of what life was like in the factories, but this was not available to the committee. In 1826 William Hall, who was sent to work in a Preston cotton mill at the age of seven, wrote:

I had to rise early and work late. . . . My orders were never to sit down during the hours of actual work. . . . I have been knocked down without warning, and brutally kicked when prostrate. . . . Once I was fifteen minutes late: for this offence I was beaten, kicked and scourged. . . . I could hardly stand when my tormentor gave over, but was instantly driven to my work.

Quoted in C. Aspin's book, *Lancashire: The First Industrial Society*, 1969

In 1815 Robert Dale Owen, the son of mill owner Robert Owen, accompanied his father on a tour of the chief textile factories. In his autobiography, published in 1874, he remembered visiting mills which:

. . . were run fifteen . . . hours a day with a single set of hands, and they . . . employ[ed] children of both sexes from the age of eight. . . . Most of the overseers openly carried stout leather thongs, and we frequently saw even the youngest children severely beaten. . . . In some

A print dating from about 1840. A poor woman, with no food in the house, sends her children out to work. In some families children were the only breadwinners

factories from one fourth to one fifth of the children were cripples or otherwise deformed, or permanently injured by excessive toil.
Robert Dale Owen: *Threading My Way*, 1874

Using the evidence

1 List the ways in which the evidence of the doctors and the others seems to contradict the evidence of the mill owners.

2 The fact that their evidence conflicts could mean:
a) that some of the witnesses were deliberately lying
b) that conditions varied from place to place
c) that similar conditions seemed different when seen by different people.
Choose which of these you think the most likely, and which the least likely. Give reasons for your answer.

3 In a cloth mill you might notice: the heat, the quality of thread produced, the noise, the smell, the state of the machinery, the quantity of thread produced, the amount of dust, how well the machines were running, the appearance of the workers, the attentiveness of the workers.
List these items (a) in the order of their importance for the owner of the mill, and (b) in the order of the impact they would make on a doctor.

4 Imagine you are about to start work as a piecer in a cotton mill. You meet a piecer who already works there. What questions would you ask him or her?

5 If you could ask an early nineteenth century mill owner why he employed children, what answers might he give?

The consequences of shorter hours

The committee asked some manufacturers what would happen if the hours of work at the mills were reduced. Adam Boyle, a Glasgow cotton spinner, told them that his workers 'would not only lose their wages for the time they lost, but we should be obliged to reduce the rates of wages'. He also thought it would be more difficult to sell his goods abroad, because a reduction in hours would increase his costs and would force him to put up his prices. Most manufacturers agreed with Boyle.

Robert Owen was the only mill owner interviewed who disagreed. He believed that it would pay mill owners to take as much care of their workers as they did of their machinery. He made sure that his workers had plenty of rest, nourishing food and good houses. Yet he made a profit. He told the committee that he thought long hours in a mill damaged the health of children. He said he did not think children under the age of ten ought to work at all, and that those over ten ought to work for only about ten hours a day. He was asked:

> *'Do you think if such an arrangement were made in regard to the number of hours, the manufacturers would suffer any loss in consequence?' — '. . . I have a firm conviction upon my mind that those articles will be produced as cheap, under the limited time and age, as they are now without limitation.'*
> *'What employment could be found for the children of the poor . . . till ten years of age?' — 'It does not appear to me that it is necessary for children to be employed under ten years of age in any regular work.'*
> *'If you did not employ them in any regular work, what would you do with them?' — 'Instruct them, and give them exercise.'*

The early career of Robert Owen	
1771	Born at Newtown in Wales. Son of local ironmonger.
1781	Left home with £2 in his pocket. Went to Stamford in Lincolnshire. Apprenticed to a draper.
1784	Left Stamford. Went to London to work for a large firm of drapers.
1785	Moved to Manchester. Borrowed £100 to set up as a machine maker. Built spinning mules. Employed men to spin on three unsold mules. Made a profit of £2 per week per mule.
1791	Appointed manager of a large Manchester spinning mill. Became famous for producing good quality yarn.
1797	Travelled to Scotland. Met Ann Dale, daughter of David Dale, owner of New Lanark Cotton Mill, one of the largest in Britain. Married Ann and then, with partners, bought New Lanark Mill from Dale.
1800	Moved to New Lanark to take charge.

Average imports of raw cotton (Millions of lb)		*Number of people employed in cotton mills* (Thousands)	
1781–9	16.9	1810	100
1790–9	29.6	1815	114
1800–9	61.7	1820	126
1810–19	105.2	1825	173
1820–9	189.6	1830	185
1830–9	354.5	1835	220

Cotton manufacturers going bankrupt (Actual numbers)		*Average value of cotton goods exported* (Thousands of £)	
1786–90	4	1780–9	760
1791–1800	49	1790–9	2 600
1801–10	141	1800–9	10 000
1811–20	102	1810–19	18 700
1821–30	113	1820–9	28 800
1831–40	227		

Using the evidence

1 Study the table of the early career of Robert Owen. What aspects of his experience before 1791 would have been useful to him as the owner of a cotton mill? For what achievement might Owen have been respected by other mill owners?

2 Most mill owners were aware of Owen's ideas on how workers should be treated. Do you think they would consider them:
a) full of sound common sense
b) liable to reduce profits
c) bound to lead to bankruptcy?
Give reasons for your answer.

3 Study the statistical tables. In what ways was the performance of the cotton industry improving? According to the tables could a mill owner look forward to:
a) expanding trade with no risk of bankruptcy
b) generally expanding trade, but with a very slight risk of bankruptcy
c) generally expanding trade, but with a real risk of bankruptcy?
How would this have influenced the mill owners when they were considering Owen's policies?

The 1819 Act

In 1819, after considering the evidence, Parliament passed an Act which laid down that:

1 No child under the age of nine should work in a cotton mill.
2 Children under the age of 16 should not work more than 12 hours a day.

To try to make sure that the Act was enforced, informers were rewarded for reporting factory owners who broke the law.

Using the evidence

1 The 1816 committee questioned mill owners, merchants, doctors and magistrates. Who else could have given them valuable evidence about working conditions in cloth mills? Can you suggest any reason why they were not consulted?

2 When they passed the 1819 Act, do you think MPs
a) paid no attention to the wishes of mill owners
b) paid some attention to the wishes of mill owners
c) paid a lot of attention to the wishes of mill owners?
Give reasons for your answer.

3 Would you expect the 1819 Act to be properly enforced? (Consider who would have known for certain that a mill owner was breaking the law. Would they have been likely to inform against him?)

4 Judging by what you have read, which of the following do you think is most likely to be true:
a) For most children, working in a cotton mill was worse than working at home under the Domestic System.
b) For most children, working in a cotton mill was better than working at home under the Domestic System.
Historians disagree about the answer to this question. Can you explain why?

5 Why do you think MPs tried to control working conditions for children in factories, but not the hours worked by children at home?

---

4 THE 1833 FACTORY ACT

The ten-hour movement

John Wood, who owned a wool-spinning factory in Bradford, agreed with Robert Owen that factory owners would be better off if they treated their workers considerately. He believed that no-one should have to work in a factory for more than ten hours a day. He tried to persuade other mill owners to reduce the hours in their mills, but they refused. So in 1830 Wood approached Richard Oastler and asked him to help.

Oastler lived at Fixby, just outside Huddersfield, where he managed the estates of a local landowner, Thomas Thornhill. Oastler knew nothing about factories, but he had just organised a successful campaign against the payment of tithes, and Wood thought that he might be able to advise him on how to win people's support for a ten-hour day in factories.

Oastler was shocked when Wood told him the long hours children had to work, and he at once took charge of the campaign for a ten-hour day. First he wrote to the local paper, *The Leeds Mercury*. In a letter published in October 1830, he pointed out that there was an outcry in Britain against black slavery in the colonies. He went on to describe conditions in Britain's factories:

> *Thousands of little children, both male and female,* but principally female, *from seven to fourteen years of age, are daily* compelled *to* labour *from six o'clock in the morning to seven in the evening, with only – Britons, blush while you read it!* – with only thirty minutes allowed for eating and recreation. *Poor infants! Ye are indeed sacrificed at the shrine of avarice. . .ye are compelled to work as long as the* necessity *of your needy parents, or the cold-blooded avarice of your worse than barbarian masters* may demand! *Ye live in the boasted land of freedom, and* feel *and mourn that* ye are slaves.

Lord Ashley as a young man. In 1851 he became Earl of Shaftesbury. He was famous for the work he did to help poor children

From now on the reformers always referred to factory children as 'white slaves'. It was a useful slogan.

With the help of George Bull, an Anglican clergyman from Byerby, an industrial parish in Yorkshire, Oastler set up 'Short Time Committees' of working men in the Yorkshire cloth-making towns. These committees organised meetings and rallies, including a 'Pilgrimage of Factory Slaves' to York. They also sent petitions to Parliament, asking for an Act to enforce a maximum ten-hour day for children.

Most supporters of the ten-hour day wanted it to apply to adults as well as children, but because they knew that most MPs still thought

Parliament had no right to limit the hours worked by grown men and women, they concentrated on the plight of boys and girls in factories. They thought that with adults and children working side by side at the same machines, any reduction in the children's hours would mean that the hours for adults would almost certainly be cut. Lord Ashley, who later became one of the leaders of the ten-hour movement, always said in his speeches that he was not concerned about the hours that adults worked. But he wrote in a letter to a friend:

> *If the labour of adults were not indirectly limited, one half of the benefits to be looked for from the [ten-hour] bill could never ensue.*

Oastler's campaign helped to raise public interest in factory reform, and in 1831 John Hobhouse, a radical MP, introduced a Bill which raised the age at which young people were allowed to work more than 12 hours a day from 16 to 18. Parliament passed the Bill. If it had been properly enforced it would have meant that no cloth mills could have operated for more than 12 hours a day. However, many manufacturers ignored it, and kept young people working for 14 or 15 hours a day.

Sadler's Bill

Meanwhile, supporters of the ten-hour movement had been preparing a Bill of their own, and on 16 March 1832 Michael Sadler MP, their spokesman in Parliament, introduced a Bill forbidding the employment of children under the age of nine in cloth factories, and allowing those between nine and 18 to work no more than ten hours a day. The House of Commons refused to pass Sadler's Bill. Instead it set up a committee to find out what conditions in factories were like.

How Sadler's committee worked

Sadler was chairman of the committee, and most of its members wanted Parliament to pass an effective law to reduce the hours of work in factories. The committee met 43 times, and examined 89 witnesses. Half of the witnesses were factory workers sent down by the Yorkshire Short Time Committees. It was the first time that factory workers had been called to give evidence to a Commons committee, and many of them must have been frightened at the thought of having to go into a room, one at a time, to be questioned by Members of Parliament, while a shorthand writer took down their answers. But Bull and Oastler told the witnesses what sort of questions to expect, and the committee members were very helpful. They asked easy, straightforward questions, and encouraged the witnesses to give details of what they and their fellow-workers suffered in the mills. The evidence which follows comes from the committee's published report, and is typical of what they heard.

A mule-spinning room. The front part of the machines – the carriages – ran backwards and forwards, guided by rails attached to the floor

The workers' evidence

Elizabeth Bentley, who was 23, came from Leeds. She told the committee that she had begun work in a flax mill at the age of six. She had worked from 5 a.m. to 9 p.m. Her main job was taking full bobbins off the machines, replacing them with empty ones. A member of the committee asked:

> *'Does that keep you constantly on your feet?' — 'Yes, there are so many frames and they run so quick . . . you have not time for anything.'*
> *'Suppose you flagged a little, or were too late, what would they do?' — 'Strap us.'*
> *'Girls as well as boys?' — 'Yes.'*
> *'Have you ever been strapped?' — 'Yes.'*
> *'Severely?' — 'Yes.'*

Elizabeth found that the dust in the room where she worked affected her lungs. As part of her work she had to pull loaded baskets across the floor. She told the committee that 'pulling the basket pulled my shoulders out of . . . place, and my ribs have grown over [them]'. As a result she was very deformed and unable to work at all.

Many witnesses were deformed. The committee interviewed a 16-year-old boy from Bradford, who had worked as a piecer in a wool mill since he was nine.

> *'What sort of a position do you stand in, in order to piece worsted goods?' — 'We have to bend our bodies and our legs.'*
> *'Have you always to bend your body?' — 'Yes, always.'*

Within a year of starting work his legs had begun to distort.

> *'Did it come on with great pain?' — 'It did.'*
> *'Will you have the goodness to show the Committee your limbs?' [The witness did so, and they appeared to be excessively crooked.]*
> *'Can you stand at all without crutches?' — 'Not without crutches, or a stick, or something to lean against.'*

Some witnesses described accidents they had seen. One saw a boy get his arm entangled in the machinery:

> *'. . . and he went up to the shafts, and both his feet were knocked off, and his left arm was dislocated at the shoulder and broken in three different places; he lived 24 hours after he got the accident, and then died.'*

Another witness said he saw:

> *'. . . a boy, who, to fettle the machine, was kneeling down, and a strap catched him about his ankles, and carried him round the wheel, and dashed his brains out on the floor.'*
> *'Do you think these accidents usually happen at the latter end of the day, when the children get tired?' — 'Yes, that boy got killed at a quarter past 7 at night.'*

The carding room. Here the cotton was prepared for spinning. The machines filled the air with dust and fluff. Workers complained that this 'stuffed their breath'

Richard Oastler summed up the feelings of the committee when he gave evidence. He told them:

> *. . . [I was once] in the company of a West Indian slave master and three Bradford spinners . . . and the spinners were obliged to be silent when the slave owner said: 'Well, I have always thought myself disgraced by being the owner of black slaves, but we never in the West Indies thought it was possible for any human being to be so cruel as to require a child of nine years of age to work twelve and a half hours a day.'*

Using the evidence

1 Look again at the piece Oastler wrote for *The Leeds Mercury*. He was a propagandist, trying to win people's support for his point of view. What does he want his readers to feel about children working in factories? What key words and expressions does he use to influence his readers?

2 Rewrite Oastler's piece so that it gives the same information but does not try to influence the feelings of the reader.

3 Design a poster advertising a meeting in favour of the ten-hour day. Try to invent an eye-catching slogan.

4 Both Elizabeth Bentley and the boy from Bradford were deformed. Do you think their deformities proved that factory

work caused children to become deformed? Give reasons for your answer. If not, was there any way the committee could have proved the point, one way or the other?

5 Imagine you are a member of the committee. Write a letter to a friend explaining how the evidence you have heard has strengthened your belief that the working day in factories must be shortened.

The committee's report

In August 1832 the committee published their report. They said the evidence showed that children were forced to work long hours and were ill-treated, and that this caused accidents and did long-term damage to their health.

Before Parliament could consider the committee's report, there was a general election. Sadler lost his seat, but Lord Ashley, MP for Dorset, had read the report. He thought it showed clearly that the Bill was needed, and when Bull asked him to take over from Sadler, he agreed. Many MPs opposed him. For example, Wilson Patten, MP for Lancashire, said that the committee had not given a fair picture. He complained that those who selected the witnesses were told 'not to send up any person on whom they could not rely; that is, as I have good reason to believe, not to send up any persons who would let out anything unfavourable to the views of the Chairman of the Committee'.

Patten pointed out that more than half of the witnesses came from Leeds; he accused some of them of lying, and said that a 'correct view' of the cloth industry nationwide 'could only be obtained by further enquiry'. He and other MPs maintained that the committee gave only the workers' point of view. They said that, to get a complete picture, the committee ought also to hear evidence from mill owners. Most MPs agreed, and in April 1833 the House of Commons appointed three commissioners to organise a nationwide enquiry into the cloth industry. They were asked to report back by July.

Using the evidence

Wilson Patten said that the committee's report was unfair. Give three or more reasons why you either agree or disagree with him. How might the fact that he was MP for Lancashire have influenced his opinion?

The 1833 Commission

The commissioners and their assistants travelled to factory towns and interviewed witnesses in private. They worked on their own, scribbling

Children working in a power-loom shop. A child looking after a couple of power looms could produce four times as much as a skilled hand-loom weaver

notes while they were interviewing, and writing them up later to send to the printer. They had several problems. One wrote:

I think it right to say that all the parties spoke such broad dialect that I was often compelled to make them repeat their answers once or twice before I could seize their meaning. Neither did they always understand me at first.

To make matters worse, some workers believed that the commissioners were biased in favour of the employers, and refused to give evidence to them. In spite of the difficulties, the commissioners finished their report in good time, and it was printed at the beginning of July.

Putting the record straight

The commissioners interviewed factory owners, and also talked to some workers who were happy in their work. For example, William Munton, aged ten, told a commissioner in Nottingham:

I have worked here half a year. I mind the teaser and pick lint. I get 3s. 6d. I was gathering 'tatoes before I came here. I got 3s. at that. When the 'tatoes were in I had nothing to do, and I came here. I have no father. This suits me very well. We have very good masters and very good overlookers here. I have never been strapped here once. It tires me standing a little now and then, but not half as much, no not a quarter as much as I used to be getting in 'tatoes with my back. I used to get leathered a deal when I was gathering 'tatoes. I like this a good deal best.

The commissioners re-examined some of the witnesses who had given evidence to Sadler's committee. Joseph Hebergam, from Huddersfield,

What does the artist who drew this picture want you to think about factory conditions in the mid-19th century?

had told the committee he met with frequent accidents at work. He now said: 'The accidents I meant were hurting my knuckles with the flies. I can't recollect that I ever saw anything worse than that.' He had also told the committee that if the overseer saw girls talking at work he would 'run and beat them the same as they beat soldiers in the barrack-yard for deserting'. Three girls who had worked with Joseph now contradicted him. They all said it was not true.

Finally, Joseph had said that in the two and a half years he had been at the mill, about a dozen children working there had died. A girl who had worked with Joseph told the commissioner: 'There was nothing like that died even while I was there, and I was there much longer than he. I only recollect two myself; there may have been more; I do not think there were.' When the commissioner asked Joseph to comment on this, he said: 'I do not remember particular how many children there were that died. I remembered better when I was in London.'

Using the evidence

1. In what respects did the commissioners' way of working differ from that of Sadler's committee?
2. On the whole, would you expect the commissioners' report to be more or less reliable than that of the committee? Give reasons for your answer.
3. List at least three ways in which William Munton thought that factory work was better than gathering potatoes. Does this necessarily mean that factory work was easy?
4. Do you think Joseph Hebergam had told Sadler's committee the truth? Give reasons for your answer.

Other evidence

Although the commissioners discovered that some of Sadler's witnesses may have been unreliable, and found some factory hands who were happy in their work, most people they interviewed gave a different impression. Here are three examples from different parts of the country. William Milner, from Bradford, told a commissioner:

> *I am going fourteen. My knees have been going about a quarter of a year. I went to work first when I was eight years old at Garnett's. Worked there from six to seven. Staid there two years. My knees did not get bent there. Went then to Duckett's, where I am now. I was then ten years old. Have had long hours there. I never felt any weakness in my knees till a quarter of a year ago, when we had long hours for the first time. They were from six to eight. My knees began to ache and bend. . . . We have from six to half past seven now. My knees are growing worse with that daily.*

Working children queue up for their pay at the end of the week

A commissioner in Manchester made the following notes while talking to a piecer:

mills: thrashes

> *Will be 15 on 6 June. His present wages are 5s. 8d. a week. Has now worked for seven years. There are five spinners and 23 piecers in the room in which he works. Five are big piecers; the rest are little ones. . . . The spinner mills the piecers with the strap many a time; mostly in the middle of the day. They mill 'em or fine 'em if too late in a morning.*

Margaret Wilson, aged 20, who worked at a flax mill in Perthshire, said:

> *. . . that she has been in a mill ever since she can recollect anything, and is now a reeler, but was formerly a spinner; that she now makes 6s. a week; that since she went to the mill she has always been hoarse and had pains in her breast, and her feet and ankles swell very much with standing so long, that she is very anxious for short hours; that she has had no time to go to the school here, that her father taught her to read some, but she can't write.*

The commissioners' report

Margaret's story was typical of most of the evidence given to the commissioners. When they wrote their report they said that, although there were only a few cases of deliberate cruelty, children did work the same hours as adults; this damaged their health, and meant that they could not get a proper education. The commissioners thought Parliament ought to act to protect these children by forbidding the employment of any child under the age of nine in factories, and limiting the working day of those between nine and 13 to eight hours, with two hours schooling a day. Young people between the ages of 13 and 18 would be able to work up to 12 hours a day – two hours longer than Ashley had proposed. The commissioners reckoned that factory owners would keep their mills open for 12 hours a day, employing two shifts of children under 13 to help operate the machines. The commissioners also proposed that full-time inspectors should be appointed to make sure that the Act was enforced.

The commissioners' report convinced most MPs that something had to be done to control the employment of children in factories, and many MPs who did not like Ashley's ten-hour Bill were quite prepared to accept the commissioners' proposals. MPs took it for granted that Ashley's Bill would have meant that adults as well as children would have been put on a ten-hour day. By following the commissioners' recommendation, they thought they could reduce the hours worked by young children without limiting the hours worked by adults, so they voted against Ashley's Bill, and defeated it. Then, on 9 August, the Chancellor of the Exchequer, Lord Althorp, proposed a Bill based on the commissioners' report. It was quickly passed by both Houses of Parliament, and on 29 August 1833 it became law. The new Act:

1 Prohibited the employment of all children under the age of nine.
2 Allowed children between the ages of nine and 13 to work up to eight hours a day, provided that they also went to school for at least two hours a day.
3 Allowed 'young persons' between the ages of 13 and 18 to work up to 12 hours a day, but did not allow them to work at night.
4 Instructed factory owners to keep a register of all the children and young persons they employed.
5 Instructed factory owners to have their premises whitewashed at least once a year.
6 Appointed four full-time inspectors to enforce the Act.

Using the evidence

1 In what way, according to the commissioners' report, was the experience of the young Manchester piecer unusual?

2 Imagine you are an MP who voted against Sadler's Bill, but voted in favour of the 1833 Act. Write a letter to a friend explaining why you opposed the former and supported the latter.

3 Would you have expected the supporters of the ten-hour day to have:
a) welcomed the 1833 Act
b) accepted the Act reluctantly
c) been violently opposed to the Act?
Give reasons for your answer.

4 Imagine you are a piecer in a cloth mill in 1830. Describe the work that you do, the way you are treated, and how you feel about the job. Base your account on the evidence you have read, and on the pictures of people at work in mills.

---

5 ENFORCING THE ACT

The inspectors' task

Robert Rickards was one of the four factory inspectors appointed to enforce the 1833 Act. With the help of five superintendents he had to inspect all the factories in the northern district, which included most of Yorkshire and Lancashire. On every visit an inspector was expected to check:

> *. . . whether any child is employed at an earlier age than the law allows; if any child or young person is employed without a certificate of age; if any child is employed for a longer time than the law allows, if the child attends school as required; if the proper time for meals is allowed, and if the interior of the mill has been whitewashed as the law directs.*

In 1833 there were 2 700 factories in Rickards' district. In August 1835 he wrote: 'Notwithstanding all that personal vigilance can effect, offences are increasing.' In 1836 he fell ill and died, worn out by work and worry.

Leonard Horner took over his district. In 1837 he wrote to the Home Secretary, Lord John Russell:

> *I now see that it is impossible for my superintendents to visit 700 factories each, twice in the year, taking into account the time they are occupied by prosecutions, in keeping their books, in making their monthly reports, and in their correspondence; and your Lordship will probably agree with me that each factory ought to be visited by a superintendent at least twice a year, in addition to the visits of the Inspector.*

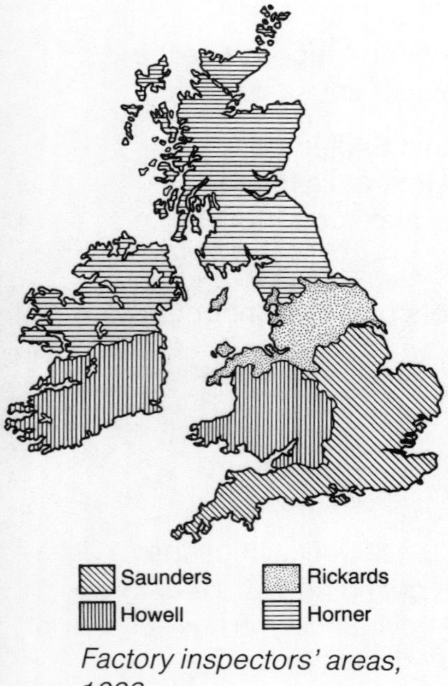

Factory inspectors' areas, 1833

The inspectors and their superintendents had to be vigilant, because the 1833 Act was very unpopular. Mill owners believed it would reduce their profits. Parents resented that the working day of children under 13 had been cut to eight hours, because it reduced the amount of money they could earn. Workers who were in favour of a ten-hour day wanted to undermine the system recommended by the commissioners, whereby two shifts or 'relays' of children under 13 would be employed, one working in the morning and one in the afternoon, leaving the adults free to work 12 or more hours a day.

Many mill owners also opposed relays. They preferred the traditional system, with children and adults working the same hours, so they dismissed all the children who were obviously under 13 years of age, and kept the rest working alongside adults for 12 hours a day.

However, in some places there were not enough children over 13 to operate the machines, so mill owners broke the law by employing children of 12 or under for a full 12-hour day. It was up to the inspectors to stop this happening.

Hiding the children

In 1838 one of the inspectors, R.J. Saunders, reported that Mr Baker, a superintendent, was looking round a mill at Ossett in Yorkshire.

> *[He] proceeded . . . into one of the rooms (where, however, the cry of 'Superintendent is coming' had already reached), and having observed two machines at work with only one boy at each, but which absolutely required two . . . he cast his eye round the room, and observed some person very busy about a bag of wool; he went up and found a boy who had been wrongly employed, in the act of being concealed therein; his head and body had been already enclosed, and the bag fastened over him, and Mr Baker only discovered him by his feet protruding.*

In May 1850 Horner visited a mill near Skipton in Yorkshire, and found nothing amiss. A few days later he received an anonymous letter stating that the owner had seen him coming and had hidden all the under-age children in the toilets. A few days later one of Horner's superintendents visited the mill with a policeman.

privies: toilets

> *He directed the constable to search the privies, and there were found in them thirteen children and young persons, male and female, packed as close together as they could lie one upon another. I need scarcely add that all of them were found to have been illegally employed in the mill.*

Leonard Horner, the factory inspector, was also an eminent scientist and an expert on education

---

Using the evidence

1 Look at the map on page 38. Why was the area allotted to Rickards much smaller than the areas allotted to the other inspectors?

2 According to Horner, did the number of factories in the northern area increase or decrease between 1833 and 1837?

3 Assuming they worked a six-day week, how many factories, on average, had Horner expected his superintendents to visit every day?

4 Which of the following would you expect to be true of mill owners in the northern area:

a) They could expect regular, thorough inspections of their mills.

b) They could expect regular, hurried visits by superintendents.

5 Do you think factory owners who employed children illegally were:
a) very likely to be found out
b) fairly likely to be found out
c) unlikely to be found out?
Give reasons for your answer.

Certificates of fitness

Mill owners were only allowed to employ children who could produce either a certificate of baptism giving their date of birth, or a doctor's certificate that they were 'of the normal strength and appearance' of a child of the legal age. This system did not work. In November 1836 Horner was in a mill at Staley Bridge near Manchester. He reported:

> *I found 13 children, certified to be 13 years of age, who measured from three feet ten inches to four feet one inch and a half, and at a mill near Macclesfield I found three with certificates of that age who measured three feet nine inches and a half, three feet ten inches, and three feet ten inches and a half. Not one of the above children looked above 11 years of age, and several were obviously not more than nine years old.*

Parents and employers had found several ways to get round the new regulations. In 1835 Rickards reported:

> *It is a common trick for parents to send children of a healthy appearance and sufficient age to a surgeon to procure a certificate, under a false name, for a younger brother or sister. Anne, for example, is sent to a surgeon for a certificate, and gives her name [as] Sarah; a certificate . . . is accordingly given in the name of Sarah . . . and Sarah, a child of ten, or perhaps nine years of age, is admitted to work in a mill for 12 hours per day.*

In October 1838 Saunders reported another trick:

> *A parent will go to one surgeon with his child, clean and in his best clothes, and if the surgeon does not think it 13, the parents immediately put on his working dress, higher shoes, and . . . will endeavour to get the child a certificate from another surgeon.*

Baptismal certificates were also unreliable. In 1840 Horner reported that he had found at Rochdale:

> *. . . a boy working with his baptismal certificate. . . . I found he had been baptised about a week before. He had been rejected by the surgeon; he went to the parish church, was baptised, an extract was given from the register and . . . the clergyman . . . put down on his certificate the statement of the parents that the boy was born so-and-so, which made him 13, of course.*

In 1836 Parliament passed an Act making it compulsory to register all births, marriages and deaths. This meant that the date of every birth was recorded on an official certificate, so it was easy to check the age of any child born after 1836.

Factory schooling

According to the 1833 Act, all children under the age of 13 who worked in mills had to go to school for at least two hours a day, six days a week. Every week they had to produce a certificate signed by the teacher before they were allowed to start work in the factory.

Some factory owners set up schools on the premises. In 1843 Saunders visited a factory school. He wrote:

> *[The teacher is] an old, disabled soldier, who has been a comber, but has long been unable to work at his trade. He now takes 35 children, and attends to some little mill work. The school room . . . is small and very dirty. When I entered the room I found three of the children employed at a winding machine, and one girl washing the floor. The remainder were sat on benches, some with an old tattered Testament on their knees, but more without.*

Testament: Bible

Thomas Howell, the inspector in charge of Wales and the West Midlands, was suspicious of all factory schools. He thought certificates provided by factory teachers were worthless because 'the schoolmaster, being in the employ of the master of the factory, is practically under his entire control'. He suspected that in many mills the children were kept at work all day, and were only transferred to the school room 'whenever the inspector or superintendent may appear at the factory lodge gate'. But he was never able to prove that this happened, and other inspectors praised some of the factory schools that they visited.

Children under 13 who worked in small mills often had to go to ordinary schools. They were not always welcome. They came straight

The school room at a large Manchester cotton mill

After 1844 working children under the age of 13 had to spend three hours a day in school. They often fell asleep in class

from work in dirty clothes, smelling of oil. They were tired, and often fell asleep in class. In some towns special schools were set up for factory children. In 1838 an inspector saw two certificates issued by such schools. One read:

> *The above Named Children has Been twelve Hours in this School after the manner of Scollers in the past week — Mary Collins.*

The other said:

> *This is to sertify that 1838 thomas Cordingley as atend martha insep school tow hours per day January 6.*

All in all the inspectors found it difficult to ensure that factory children below the age of 13 were being properly educated.

Using the evidence

1 Horner was sure that many of the children working in the factories were in fact under age. Did this necessarily mean that the surgeons who gave them their certificates were stupid or dishonest? Give reasons for your answer.

2 What evidence is there to suggest that some surgeons did not check children carefully before granting certificates?

3 Imagine you are a factory inspector in 1840 who has been asked why it is difficult to ensure that factory children are being properly educated. Give at least three reasons in reply.

A factory inspector checking the names and ages of the children

Punishments imposed

In his report to the Home Secretary in March 1837, Horner gave details of what happened to mill owners who broke the law. He wrote:

> *My superintendents, in a large proportion of instances where they found things wrong, were satisfied by assurances that there was no intention to break the law, and by promises that it should be strictly attended to in future; but there were unfortunately too many cases where . . . there was evidently a wilful disregard of the statute. . . . It has [therefore] been necessary to institute many prosecutions. . . . In the quarter ending the 31st of March, there have been 177.*

Horner was disappointed to find that magistrates often treated mill owners who broke the law very leniently. In one quarter 245 out of 362 convictions were punished by fines of £1 or even less. He gave examples:

> *The magistrates at Kendal fined a mill-occupier 20s. for overworking children, and two others, who had not required the children to attend school as provided by the Act, were fined 5s. each. A firm who had not*

given their workers the time for their meals as required by the Act were fined 20s., although on inspecting their mill myself not two months before, I had accepted their alleged excuse of ignorance, had warned them . . . and had received a promise of amendment.

The Kendal magistrates had also fined a mill owner 2s. 6d. for failing to whitewash his mill.

It was stated that the mill was in a dirty condition. If this obligation of yearly whitewashing be considered a proper precaution . . . it is obvious that the penalty, in a clear case of neglect, ought at least to equal the expense of the process.

In 1836 Howell submitted a list of all the convictions in his area for offences against the 1833 Act, and the fines imposed:

Place	*Nature of offence*	*Fine*
Trowbridge, Wiltshire	Allowing a child under 13 years of age to remain in his mill without the certificate of a surgeon	£1
Blanchestown, Co. Dublin	Employing a child under 13 years of age more than 48 hours in the week, and more than nine hours in the day	£10
Llandaff, Glamorgan	Overworking children under 13 years of age, no certificates of age, no time book	None
Caerphilly, Glamorgan	Same as last	£1
Ditto	Ditto	£1
Ditto	Overworking children under 13 years of age, no registers or time books	£1
Kidderminster, Worcs.	Employing a child . . . more than nine hours without a certificate . . . that she was 13 years of age	£5
Ditto	Allowing a child under 13 years of age to remain in their mill without the certificate of a surgeon or physician	10s.
Caldwell Mill, Worcs.	Employing a girl 16 years of age . . . more than 69 hours a week	10s.
Bridgnorth, Shropshire	Employing a child under 13 years of age without the certificate of a surgeon	£1
Welshpool, Montgomery	Same offence as above	£1
Ditto	Ditto	£1

Carrying loads of clay in a brickworks was harder work than piecing in a cotton mill

In their later reports, the inspectors noticed that fewer mill owners were breaking the law. In January 1840 Horner still thought that a few children under 13 were illegally employed, but he went on:

> *The chief evils that formerly existed have been remedied to a great extent, and therefore . . . the Act has been productive of much good.*

Using the evidence

Study the table of prosecutions in Howell's district.

1. What was the commonest offence for which mill owners were prosecuted?
2. On the whole do the magistrates seem to have dealt with offending mill owners
   a) leniently
   b) severely
   c) very severely?
3. What other information would you need to have to be able to tell if the magistrates had dealt fairly with a particular case?
4. Does the table give you enough information to be able to tell if the mill owners in Howell's area were more or less law abiding than those in Horner's area? If not, what additional information do you need?
5. Imagine you are a superintendent inspecting factories after 1833. Write a diary of a week's work, including accounts of incidents you might have seen on factory visits and in the magistrates' courts.

6

THE END OF THE STRUGGLE

The inspectors' reports encouraged MPs to extend the 1833 Act, and between 1842 and 1867 Parliament passed nine major Acts to improve working conditions in factories and mines.

Acts affecting cloth mills	
1844	Act allowed children of eight to work in mills, but reduced the hours of work for children under 13 to 6.5 a day. It limited the hours of work for women to 12 a day, and ordered that dangerous machinery should be fenced in.
1847	Act limited the hours of work for women and young persons to ten a day.
1850	Act prohibited the use of relays of women and young persons. Increased the working day to 10.5 hours.

Acts affecting other industries	
1842	The Mines Act made it illegal for children under ten and all women to work underground.
1845	The Factory Act was extended to cover calico printing works. . . .
1860	. . . bleaching and dyeing . . .
1861	. . . and lace-making. (Also during this year a commission was appointed to inquire into the employment of children in all trades and industries.)
1864	The Factory Act was extended to cover match-making, pottery and cartridge-making . . .
1867	. . . and all factories employing 50 or more people.

Horner was particularly pleased that the 1844 Act required machinery to be fenced in. In 1845 he wrote:

> *When I view the complicated machinery amongst which people work, the infinite number of wheels and other mechanisms with projections to catch, sharp edges to cut, and vast weights to crush, the crowded state in which machines are often packed together, and the great velocity and force with which they move, it often appears a marvel to me that accidents are not of daily occurrence in every mill.*

A girl and two young women winding cotton yarn in about 1870

Results of the Factory Acts

In 1833 Mark Phillips, MP for Manchester, told the House of Commons that if factories were limited to a ten-hour day 'for two years, or even for one year, at the end of that time the [cotton] trade would be wholly gone from this country, and would be in the hands of foreigners'. Philip Howard, MP for Carlisle, agreed. He said 'the trade would be unable to cope with foreign competition, and nothing but ruin would be the consequence'.

The following table shows the average quantity of cotton cloth, in millions of yards, exported from Britain between 1810 and 1859:

1810–19	227
1820–9	320
1830–9	553
1840–9	978
1850–9	1855

One of the reasons that production increased was that improved looms and spinning machines were installed in mills, but James Grant, manager of a Glasgow cotton mill, thought that the employees worked better too. In 1838 he told James Stuart, a factory inspector:

> *... that the piecers above 13 years old answer for every purpose at this factory perfectly well.... That he ... performed the same work when he was 8 years old ... and as he was employed 12 hours or more, he was sometimes tired; but he never hears of the piecers now complaining of fatigue, as they are so much older and stronger.*

Shorter hours certainly benefited the mill workers. In 1868 W. Abram, a Lancashire journalist, remembered how in 1843 he used to watch the workers coming home from the factories 'smeared with oil and grime ... sickly and wan ... prematurely broken down and decrepit'. But by 1868 all this had changed. He wrote:

> *Sickness and mortality have been reduced to an extent that is almost incredible. Deformity of body is now a rare exception.... The young men and maidens employed in the mills are as robust as the families of the indolent classes.*

The workers were also better off financially because, 'thanks mainly to accelerated machinery and improved methods of working', their wages had increased, so they could afford good food and 'moderately comfortable' houses.

Leonard Horner found that people knew who they had to thank for better working conditions. In 1853 he wrote:

> *I have again and again heard those who knew the state of the children in factories prior to 1833 and contrast it with what it is now, bless the*